Financial
26 Things
to Teach your
Parents

by Marlena Jareaux

INSPIRED
BY THE
BEACH
PUBLISHING

The saving man becomes the free man.

— Chinese proverb

*He is rich or poor according to what he is,
not according to what he has.*

—Henry Ward Beecher

One of my favorite sayings is "If you want something different, than do something different." So it is to you, my son, that I dedicate this book. I want you to be armed with the education that can empower you to make wise choices for your future. My teacher was the school of hard knocks, Life, and the consequences of my actions due to my ignorance. Forever the mom (a career path that I chose and would choose again if I had to do it all over), I'm once again hoping to save you from the mistakes that I made. Will you and your friends listen...?

Mom

Cover design by Jennifer Arbaiza Graphic Design.

Illustrations by Rusty Haller.

Page design and typesetting by JustYourType.biz.

Printed in the United States of America.

Publisher's Cataloging-in-Publication data

Jareaux, Marlena C.
  26 financial things to teach your parents / by Marlena Jareaux.
  p. cm.
  1st edition.
  ISBN 978-0-9790415-2-5
1. Youth--Finance, Personal--Juvenile Literature. 2. Financial literacy--United States-- Juvenile Literature. 3. High school students --United States--Finance, Personal--Juvenile Literature. 4. Consumer education--Juvenile literature. I. Title. II. Twenty six financial things to teach your parents.

HG179 .J31 2008
640.73--dc22   2008923647

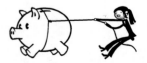

Table of Contents

Why YOU Should Read This Book...

Message for teens/tweens:

Being a person between the ages of 11 and 17 isn't easy. I'm sure that you already know that by now. It can seem like no one understands you (except for your friends), and that your parents or guardians have no idea what it is like to be in YOUR shoes. The world is very different in some ways than it was when your parents/guardians were growing up in it, so you may be thinking that they don't know what it's like to grow up in THIS world. I can assure you that though things may look so different, there are many things that are true for you that were the same for your parents when they were your age. One thing is very different. The availability of information is far greater and is easier to access than it ever was for your parents (or their parents). Today, you need only connect to the internet through your home computer, school computer or library's computer in order to access most of the information that you would need or be interested in finding. In that area, you have it much easier than your parents did. That's one of the reasons why you are so important in and to this world. Let me explain.

Many of your parents and guardians did not have access to the internet when they were growing up. Some of them still don't use the internet. Fine, no problem. That's where you can help them. Many of your parents/guardians want to get information on doing things, buying things, investing in things, and where to find things, but they might not know how (or have the time to do it). That's one of the ways that you can put your computer and internet researching skills to great use. But even if you don't have the greatest computer skills or have access to the internet, you can still help. Personal financial education (the teaching of everything that has to do with money and financial wealth) was probably NOT taught to your parents when they were growing up. There are many people who are trying to change that in your schools right at this moment. Some of you may have already had a class about money, saving and budgeting but a lot of you haven't. Don't feel bad though, because like I said, your parents may not have either. That's why this book exists.

Do you want to be a millionaire? Do you know how? Do you know how an ATM or bank card gives you money from the machine? Have you ever wondered why some people have credit cards, and some can't? Do you think that credit cards allow you to tap into free money? Did you know that credit cards can help you, or they can drag you down into the mud? Do you know what a <u>budget</u> is? How about <u>interest</u>?

If your parents or teachers haven't talked to you about any of these things yet, then I'm reaching you at the right moment in your life: The moment before you may make a serious financial mistake that can cost you lots of money, sadness and distress in your future. It doesn't have to be that way though. Just like you learned how to put the 26 letters of the alphabet together so that you could spell your name and put it and other words onto homework assignments or a college/job application, you must learn about money, bills, credit and savings so that you can put it all together to help create the life that you want for yourself. So this book is for YOU. May it help you to learn the many things about money and wealth (not just that you need it to buy what you want) that your parents may not have taught you or learned themselves. It is my hope that you will give the benefit of some of your new-found knowledge to your parents, who did the best that they could with what they had. It's not too late for them, despite the fact that they are older than you. You're never too old to start doing something new, so please help your parents, guardians and adults in your life by sharing this information with them. The future of our world, and of humanity, depends on what YOU do in it. There is enough for everyone, so please share.

Wishing you prosperity in your future,
Marlena

Message for parents/guardians/adults:

This is one book that I definitely could have used when I was growing up. I say that because I made some of the most horrible financial decisions and mistakes beginning right after high school and going into my twenties. I'm pretty sure that I made those mistakes because I just didn't know any better. No one really told me about the importance of saving or credit, or about investing in stocks or buying a house. I do remember hearing from my parents "Save some of that money", but I don't think that I ever understood why they were saying it, or why I should do it. So I didn't. I don't blame my parents though, because I'm not sure if they were told by their parents either. When it came time for me to raise my own son, I realized that there was a great deal that I had learned about credit, saving and investing from the "school of hard knocks". I wanted him to have that knowledge and be able to use it sooner than I was able. So I am writing this book in the hopes that he will "get" some of the important, time-tested principles that are contained in this book.

Many things are different in my son's generation, especially when you compare them to life as it was for me growing up in York, Pennsylvania in the 1960s. I'm sure that you feel the same way. I don't believe that there were as many stories of people either being millionaires or going bankrupt back in the 60's as there are today. If you turn on the TV today, you are likely to see shows about people competing to have the chance to marry a millionaire; news stories about people who have won millions in the lottery or lost everything they owned due to bad choices or fate; or game shows that test either your skills in answering questions or your intuition in selecting "the right briefcase" in the hopes that you will win a million dollars. Growing up, I watched Maxwell Smart and Agent 99 try to foil the evil plans of Siegfriend and KAOS; dreamed of what I would wish for if I had a genie like the one in I Dream of Jeannie™; and picked up a pointer or two about the true costs of items as I watched the contestants of The Price Is Right try to out-guess each other on the prices of things in the hopes that they'd be able to go home with a year's supply of them. Some things only appear to have changed, but really haven't when you scratch beneath the surface. As I child I walked to the neighborhood store to buy an ice cream cone for 10¢, but earning that 10¢ was sometimes challenging. It's the same for my son now, except that same ice cream cone is now $1.25. It's just as hard for him to get his $1.25 today as it was for me to get the 10¢ back then. Something else that hasn't changed: many kids still live for the "here and now" with little thought of the consequences and the future. Maybe I did too... I'll have to ask my parents. Is that really any different than the "get it now, pay later" mentality that is so prevalent in our society today?

Many parents and adults were told as children that it was rude to talk about money and finances. When many of us grew up and had children of our own, we decided to shield them and only show them that we were strong and know all of (or most of) the answers about life. But I've come to discover that it can do more damage than good to have my son living starry-eyed and ignorant to the financial truths of the world that we live in. Open any magazine or turn on any TV and you are bound to see a celebrity, star or pro sports player of some sort who is showcasing the 10 cars that they own, the huge diamond(s) on their hand or around their neck, or one of the many houses around the world that they are able to jet off to in a moment's notice. I knew I had to do something when I saw a story about a star who had her nail stylist cut up what I think were $20 or $100 bills in order to cover (and style) her fingernails. Geez, does she go to the salon every week, and when did nail polish go out of style? I want to ask you: If you aren't teaching your children finances, then who is?

Are your children being taught to live an extravagant lifestyle, or one that demonstrates responsible money and wealth management? If you leave it up to chance and outside influences like the media images that are all around us telling us to spend, Spend, SPEND, you will be making a mistake that could cost your kids handsomely in the form of a potentially disastrous financial future.

People often learn by example. They also learn by seeing and hearing about the mistakes and successes that other people make/have and any resulting consequences and benefits that they receive. Your kids are watching and learning from you and every one of your financial actions. What are you teaching them that you may not be aware of? Do you know how difficult it is to see in the dark? Don't be the one that keeps your kids in the dark when they're looking for you to guide them to the light.

To you and your kids' financial prosperity (with the lights on)...

MJ

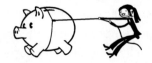

Author's note/disclaimer:

I hope that this book will be helpful for you. Information contained in this book is provided for informational purposes only. It is not intended to be a substitute for any advice that you may receive from a professional financial advisor. Each person's circumstances may be different, and may warrant a different approach than the one given in this book. The publisher and author specifically disclaim any liability from any damages (whether direct or indirect, special, general or consequential) or loss which is incurred as a consequence, directly or indirectly, of the use or application of any of the contents of this publication, which contents are provided "AS IS".

Internet addresses and telephone numbers given in this book were accurate at the time it went to press.

Definitions:

Here are a few definitions that you may find to be useful to you as you are reading this book.

ATM: Automated Teller Machine that allows customers of a financial institution to do financial transactions at a location that doesn't require a human being.

Bill: A statement of charges for bills or services.

Creditor: One to whom money is owed.

Debt: Something owed, as money, goods or services.

Expenses: Something requiring the expenditure of money.

Income: Money or its equivalent received in exchange for labor or services, from the sale of goods or property, or as profit from financial investments.

Wealth: A great quantity of money or valuable possessions; riches; abundance.

Financial
26 Things
to Teach your
Parents

Learn more so you can earn more.

Despite the fact that I like to learn many things (and thank goodness there is no limit to the number of things out there to learn), it wasn't always that way. When I was younger, I used to ask my parents why I had to go to school. I didn't understand what geometry or physics had to do with my life, and didn't see the point in going to school day after day to learn them or about the mixing of chemicals in chemistry class. Back then, I was told that it was simply the law and that I had to go to school. At some point, I learned that school wasn't just a distraction to keep me busy and out of the house as I had suspected. I learned that school was for my betterment and greater good. The definition of "betterment" is "an improvement" (The American Heritage Dictionary, 1983, p. 67). Those of you who have read the book <u>26 Things to Teach Your Parents</u> know that I have the following to say about dictionaries: "…that's right, I had to look in a dictionary to be able to give you this definition, and it won't kill you to open up one every now and then so that you can be clear on what a word means…I've had this one for the past 20 years and I still use it." (p.21).

Before you start thinking that the point of this chapter is to get you to stay in school and go to college, let me say right now that it's not. Despite the many benefits of going to college (too many to mention here), history is filled with stories of the successes of many men and women who did not finish or even complete one day of college. Before you start getting excited thinking that this chapter is a permission slip for you not to go to college, hold your horses for a moment. You may very well make a great success of your life without stepping foot into a college classroom. That remains to be seen. But know this: most of the financially secure people in the world kept on learning long after the required schooling was over. Learning doesn't just happen in classrooms.

❖ You might learn a new way of doing something by working on a team with other people.

❖ You can learn a new way of solving a problem by reading in a book how someone else solved a similar problem.

❖ You may watch your friend do something in a way that you hadn't thought of, and decide to give it a try.

There is a saying: If you learn what you've always learned, you'll think what you've always thought, and you'll do what you've always done, and then you'll get what you've always gotten.

The world is changing all around us every day. That means that the same things that worked to solve yesterday's problems may not work when solving today's problems. The person who keeps learning the ways that the world is changing, and learns new and different ways to create solutions to those problems, will be the person who gets rewarded by the people who are looking for those solutions.

Take a look at your television or the computer that you use at home or at school. Does the screen show things in color? A while ago, TVs and computer screens used to show pictures in black and white. If they broke down, they were repaired by someone who knew how to fix them. Let's say that Wally knows how to fix black and white screens, but never wanted to learn how to fix color ones. Would your family call him to fix the screens in your home? Ask your parents if they or their boss would call him to fix the screens in the office. Sadly, Wally would not be called upon very often to fix any screens because the information that he knows is outdated and not very useful. And if he's not getting called, then he's probably not getting paid. Hopefully, Wally knows how to do other things.

Keep learning so that you can keep earning.

Pay yourself first.

One of the most powerful things that you can do in order to build wealth (riches and prosperity) is also easy to do. When you sit down each month to pay your bills, set an amount aside and have that be the first "payment" that you make from the money that you earned. Get in the habit of making that payment to yourself be the very first thing that you do with the money that you earn. You must treat yourself the same way that you treat any of the other people that you owe money to (creditors). Decide on a monthly amount, and stick with it no matter what. If you find that you don't have enough money in order to pay for all of your bills, the answer is not to stop paying yourself. The answer is to either do one of two things (or both): you must increase your income or decrease your expenses (bills). Perhaps it's not so important to have a latte or ice cream sandwich EVERY day. Or maybe there is some extra work you can do to earn more money (or you can work extra hours at your job). Why is it so important to pay yourself first?

Many times, when a person gets a paycheck, this is what happens to the money: First, they take care of their immediate expenses and bills, and then they consider the rest of the money to be disposable money that they can spend as they wish until their next batch of money comes in. When you think about it, there is ALWAYS something that you could think of to spend your money on, right? If the money is easily available for spending, there's a good chance that you will spend it (unless you have great self-control and can tuck it away). So when you pay yourself first, let's say 5-10% of your paycheck as an example, you should immediately put that money into an account for safe-keeping. If 5-10% seems high to

you right now, you can start with as little as $5 per paycheck just to get you into the habit of saving. (Some people say to pay yourself the first hour of your income each day). You then can take care of your expenses and bills, while having some money left over to spend as you wish (though maybe not as much as you would have under the old way). Is that really such a bad thing when the benefit to you is having money waiting for you for a rainy day? More on the "rainy day" later.

You can ask your employer or boss to automatically put a certain amount of your paycheck each month into a savings account. That way, you don't even have to think about it or remember to do it. What a surprise you will have when you periodically peek into that account and find that your balance is growing nicely. Doesn't matter how you do it, but just remember that YOU and your future are just as important as any of your bills. Put yourself in front of the line and pay yourself first!

$100 in a box is still $100.
$100 in the bank is not.

A bank account is a fund that you set up with a bank or credit union. You are able to make deposits and withdrawals from that account whenever you wish. Deposits are all of the checks, cash and electronic transfers that you ask to have put into your account that increases the amount of your account balance. When you withdraw money out of your account, you are taking money out (which decreases the amount of your balance). You can go to the bank to withdraw money, write a check that tells the bank to give someone else the money, use a debit card (looks like a credit card), or use your ATM card to take cash out by going to an ATM machine. When you deposit cash or get an electronic deposit, you can have use of that money immediately. When you deposit a check, your bank may wait to make the money available for you to use until it is sure that the bank's name that is written on the check sends the money to your bank. When you go to your bank to take out money, it immediately gets removed from your balance. When you use an ATM or debit card, the money is put on hold in your account, which means that it's still there, but is not available for you to use because your bank is getting ready to send it to someone else. When you write a check to someone else, they have to deposit it with their bank (and they will have that same wait time) or they can actually go to your bank and ask for the money (if they have a photo ID to prove who they are).

There are many different types of accounts, but the two main ones discussed here are the savings account and checking account. A savings account is mostly used to store money that you don't plan on spending in the near future. You can't write a check from a savings account, but you can have an ATM card or go to the bank to make withdrawals (usually a limit to how many withdrawals you can do in a month though). In exchange for you having slightly less access to your money, the bank will pay you interest (more money) for having your money available to them. A checking account is used to hold money that you think you will have to spend sometime soon. Checking accounts don't usually pay you any interest because the bank knows that the money in that account probably isn't going to be there long. A check is an actual piece of paper with your name, address and account number on it that looks like a permission slip. If you want to give a person or company some money, you write their name on the "pay to the order of" line, write the date, write the amount of money that you want to give them, and sign your name on the bottom. A check is like a "promise to pay" to a person or company for the amount of money written on the check. Here's what a check looks like:

Your name	Date: _____
Your street address	
Your city, state, zip	

Pay to the order of: _____ *[Your creditor]* _____ | $40.00 |

_____Dollars

| Name of |
| your bank |

Phone bill   *[Your signed name]*

Memo   Signature

ACCOUNT NUMBER PRINTED ON CHECK

There are many great benefits to having an account at a bank or credit union. First, it is safer to have your money there than having it sit around your house, under your mattress or in your piggy bank. Not only is it more likely to get taken from a house, but it's also more likely to get spent. The less cash that you have around, the less likely it will be that you will spend it. Out of sight, a little less out of mind. Also, when it comes to having your paycheck cashed, it is usually less expensive to have your check converted to money using your bank account than it will be if you use a check cashing company. Check cashing companies charge you a percentage of your paycheck amount in order to exchange it for money. Depending on your location, they can charge anywhere from 1% to 4% of your paycheck amount. So if you have a $500 paycheck, the check cashing place can charge you up to $20 or more to change it into cash. If you get paid twice a month, that becomes $40. Compare that to the fees that your bank may charge you to have an account with them. It would be rare to have a bank charge $40 each month (or even half of that) to have an account open with them. In fact, a lot of banks and credit unions don't charge anything to have an account open with them. As I mentioned above, banks and credit unions actually pay YOU to have some accounts open with them. Your mattress or piggy bank won't do that.

*Note: Having a checking account is a privilege. You will receive checks, like the one above, that will allow you to buy things from stores simply by writing them a check to pay for them. The store won't know whether or not you have in your account the amount of money that you write on the check. Make sure that you do. If you write a check to someone knowing that you don't have the money in your account, it is a crime in a number of States: A crime that can get you sent to jail. Banks will not give part of the amount on the check: It's all or nothing. Make sure the bank can pay out the amount that you wrote on the check. "Bouncing a check" (gets bounced back and not paid) will cost you money (bank will charge you). If you make a habit of doing it, the bank can close your account and report your behavior to a credit bureau, making it difficult for you to find a bank willing to let you open another account. More on credit bureaus later.

Money doesn't grow on trees.

Almost everyone has heard this before from someone in their lives. Everyone can look outside at trees and see for themselves that money clearly does not grow from any of them. And though that fact may be obvious, there are many people who go through life spending money as if they have an unlimited supply of it. Most times when someone says that money doesn't grow on trees, what they are trying to say is that it is not always easy to earn money, which means you must watch how you spend your money because it is valuable. There are several ways that you will get money in your lifetime. You will either earn it, get it as a gift, get it from your family, win it, or find it (hopefully, you won't steal it). For most people, their main source of getting it will be to earn it. Producing money from a job or a business is not the only way that you can earn money.

Despite the fact that money does not grow on trees, you can make it grow at a rate that's almost as fast as a tree growing. Before you say "That's not very fast", let me tell you that there are willow and poplar tree hybrids that grow 14-20 feet in a year's time. Once you start paying yourself first and saving money in an account (preferably one that earns interest), you can start to see the real power that interest can have. Here's what happens when interest gets compounded onto your bank balance. Let's say that you start off with $1000 in a bank account. Let's also say that your bank pays 4% in interest, and that they compound (added back on top of) the interest 4 times a year. Each time that they pay you interest for having your money in the bank, they add the interest onto your bank balance. So the first time that it happens, you can expect somewhere close to $10 to be added to your balance. This brings your new balance to $1010. The

next time that interest is calculated and paid to you, it will be based on $1010, which means that your interest will now be $10.10 and get added to the balance making it now $1020.10. This keeps happening until you take your money out of the bank. So if you left $1000 in that bank account and didn't touch it, it would grow to $1488.86 in 10 years. Not bad for not doing anything but leaving your money alone and untouched.

If you ever want to find out how long it will take to double your initial investment (money), you can use the Rule of 72 to figure it out. The formula is 72/interest rate=amount of time. So if you start with $4000 and want to find out how long it will take to double that amount when earning 6% interest, you would take that magic number 72 and divide it by 6. The answer would be about 12 years. If the interest rate is 10%, the number of years changes to 7.2. You can use the same formula if you want to find out what interest rate you'd have to have in order to double your money in a certain amount of time. If you want to double your money in 6 years, you take the number 72 and divide it by 6. The answer "12" tells you that you would have to earn a 12% interest rate.

This is a very simple formula that can help you to make some important financial decisions. Please share it with your parents.

Slow and steady usually wins the race.

You may have heard the story of the tortoise and the hare. The tortoise is a turtle, and the hare is a rabbit. When you think of a turtle and a rabbit having a race against each other, most people would guess that the rabbit (hare) would be the favored winner. Hares are fast and hop all over the place, while turtles are not because they slowly crawl. In the story, the hare takes off running at a fast pace. It isn't long before he decides to take a break on the side of the road. He looks back at the tortoise and asks him how he expects to win the race when he is walking so slowly. The hare ends up getting sleepy. He decides that he has plenty of time to take a nap since the tortoise is so slow, so he does. The tortoise walked and walked until he not only passed the sleeping hare, but also crossed the finish line. It wasn't until the other animals in the forest cheered loudly for the tortoise's victory that the hare woke up. He ran as fast as he could towards the finish line, but it was too late. Slow and steady had won the race!

You can do the same with the saving and investing of money. Be sure to let your parents know that it is never too late to start saving. Something saved beats nothing saved any day. You can take a small amount of money and turn it into a large amount of money with enough time and with the right rate of return. It's also never too early to start saving. In fact, the sooner you start to save, the more money you will have later for when you will need or want it. Here is a chart that demonstrates what happens if two people decide to save money but start at different times. One person starts saving $1000 per year early (age 22) and then stops at age 29 (but doesn't touch the money), and the other person doesn't start until they are 30 years old and keeps going until age 65.

Age	Person 1	Growth	Person 2	Growth
22	1,000	1,100	0	0
23	1,000	2,310	0	0
24	1,000	3,641	0	0
25	1,000	5,105	0	0
26	1,000	6,716	0	0
27	1,000	8,487	0	0
28	1,000	10,436	0	0
29	1,000	12,579	0	0
30	0	13,837	1,000	1,100
31	0	15,221	1,000	2,310
32	0	16,743	1,000	3,641
33	0	18,418	1,000	5,105
34	0	20,259	1,000	6,716
35	0	22,285	1,000	8,487
36	0	24,514	1,000	10,436
37	0	26,965	1,000	12,579
38	0	29,662	1,000	14,937
39	0	32,628	1,000	17,531
40	0	35,891	1,000	20,384
61	0	265,600	1,000	221,252
62	0	292,160	1,000	244,477
63	0	321,376	1,000	270,024
64	0	353,514	1,000	298,127
65	0	388,865	1,000	329,039
	Total at completion	$388,865	Total at completion	$329,039
	Less Total Contributions	$(8,000)	Less Total Contributions	$(35,000)
	Net Earnings	$380,865	Net Earnings	$294,039

The rate of return that is earned for each of them is 10%. Person #1 contributed a total of only $8000, and left the money alone. Person #2 contributed a total of $35,000 and also left the money untouched (but got a later start). Though Person #2 contributed more money, their ending balance was $85,000 less than Person #1 who deposited less money (but started saving earlier). A strong argument for the benefits of getting an early start to saving.

One of the best pieces of advice with saving is to put it on auto-pilot. That means to set it up so that it happens automatically, and then let it do its' thing. Having money go automatically to your savings account is good. Having money automatically taken out of an account in order to buy mutual funds or stocks can be great. The amount that you set aside for savings or investing might even be small, but every little bit has the ability to add up to become something bigger that will help you to win the race in the end. Please share the above chart with your parents.

Make your money work for you.

So far we've learned about earning money, the importance of paying yourself first, the value of deposit accounts, and the significance of saving (even at a slow and steady pace). It is also important to be able to make your money work for you. There are many ways to help make sure that your money is going as far as it can possibly go.

First, you can do some "shopping around" to make sure that your money is getting treated fairly and in the best way possible. That means that you should <u>not</u> just put your money into a savings account at the bank across the street simply because it is across the street. Banks and credit unions offer different services and different rates. You should check at least two different banks (if not more) to ensure that you are getting the best rate for your money. One bank could offer an account that pays 1% interest (but have no minimum required balance), while another could offer 4% (but require you to keep a $300 minimum). Banks and credit unions also differ in the fees that they charge for having the account. Some charge monthly fees, while others don't. Monthly fees can add up over time and eat away at your account balance, unless you can obey the account rules in order to avoid fees. So choose wisely.

Even when you do decide on a bank or credit union that you want to use, you should check from time to time to see if they have any new products or accounts that can serve you better. When your account balances grow, so will your options. When they see that you are a responsible accountholder and that you are serious about growing your money, the doors of opportunity will open up to you. There are other

types of savings accounts that are available (that pay larger interest rates). You'll get introduced to them as you continue down your path to financial prosperity.

The same thing is true of investing in stocks and mutual funds. A share of stock represents actual ownership in a company. You may own one share of stock, or millions of shares. You won't be the only one who has stock in the company, so if you own one share of stock, your "share" of the company will not be as large as the person who has many. A share of stock can cost any amount of money. It could cost $1 or $10,000. As a stock investor, you earn money on stocks when dividends (profit payments) are given to stockholders or when the stock price goes up (higher than the amount that you bought it). You buy stock through a stock broker (person who can buy & sell stock for you or give advice about it), through an online stock company, or through the company itself. It's important to note that you can also lose money if the price of the stock drops to an amount that is lower than the price that you paid. I encourage you to do research on investing before actually doing it. There is a lot to know about buying and selling stocks, and because of the money at stake, it should never be considered a game.

Money in your bank account is protected by insurance, for at least $100,000. Stocks and mutual funds are not insured, so if the value goes down for a stock, it will be your loss if you need to sell the stock at that lowered price. If you bought a stock for $40 a share and the company has a major setback (causing the stock price to fall to $15 per share) but you need to sell your shares, there is no way to get your $40 per share back. Whatever the stock price is on the day that you want to sell is the amount that you will get. There are many people who have made significant amounts of money with the buying and selling of stocks. There are many stories of people buying stock at $50 per share, and having it rise to $240 per share (and selling it to get the profit). There are many people who buy shares of stock from money out of every one of their paychecks (auto-pilot investing), and look at their account value ten years later to discover that they are a millionaire! But just as there are stories of gain, there are stories of loss also. There is risk involved, so the stock market is not to be taken lightly. Mutual funds are a collection of different stocks and bonds that are bought by a company so that investors can buy shares in that collection and risk. One share in a mutual fund may have 20 different stocks in it. There are many mutual funds that exist, so research is strongly suggested so that you know what stocks are in the funds and the fees that come with investing in those funds. Investing in mutual funds is thought to be less risky than stocks because the risk is spread out between many different stocks (whether the fund does good is not tied to the performance of any one stock). There are many options for investing. Again, please do your research. You could perhaps start with your parents and ask them if they have done any stock or mutual fund investing, and how it worked out for them.

No matter where you decide to "park" your hard-earned money, periodically check to make sure that it's still the best option for you. The day may come when you decide to stop working to earn money. When and if that day comes, you will have the money that you made combined with the money that your money made for you. Make informed choices.

There will always be a rainy day coming.

It is the case in most places in the world that it's going to rain. There are some places that get more rain than others. Both the State of Washington and the State of Oregon each get lots of rain. Other places in the world go weeks or months at a time before they see any rain. The point is: rain is coming, someday. So it would be crazy to have a house with no roof on it. Along with the many dangers that having no roof would bring, rain falling into the house could destroy your possessions, carpet, furniture and the house itself. Though we are able to sometimes predict when the rain is coming, we as humans can't control it. Like it or not, we have to deal with it.

The same is true for life. There will be things that happen that you won't be able to see coming or have any control over. Some examples are:

- ❖ Car accident or breakdown
- ❖ Medical or dental emergency
- ❖ Lost or stolen coat needing to be replaced
- ❖ Loss of a job (but your bills keep coming in)
- ❖ Anything you didn't expect

One thing is clear. You should expect the unexpected. That way you won't be caught off-guard when unexpected events happen. You'll be prepared for the unexpected by having a "rainy day" fund available. It needs to be money that you can easily get to in case you need to spend it. This wouldn't be money that is invested in stocks or mutual funds. It would be money that is tucked away in a savings account (making it harder to spend since it's not in your house) that would take a simple trip to the bank for you to reach it.

Still don't see the need for a rainy day fund? Imagine that you make $2000 per month. Your bills add up to $1300 per month, and you spend another $600-700 per month on gas, food, movies and everything else you want. Hopefully you are saving some of the money for your future as was mentioned earlier in this book. Now what happens if your car breaks down two months from now and the repair bill comes to $1000 (not an unreasonable amount given the expense of cars)? How will you get the car fixed? Will you have the money?

There's a better chance that you'll be prepared for rainy days if you have a rainy day fund. The question is not if a rainy day is coming, but when.

You CAN have it all, but do you NEED to?

Whatever it is that you want in life is possible for you to have: A loving family, a successful career, financial riches… anything and everything. Whatever it is that you can dream and think of can be yours if you truly want it and are willing to do the work that is necessary in order to achieve it. The things that are handed to you easily and without any work on your part won't usually be the things that are the most memorable for you. The things that you have to work hard to get or keep (or both) are the things that you will most likely appreciate the most. As long as you are willing to do the work for the things that you most desire in your life, you can have them all.

Having that knowledge that you can have anything that you want in life is powerful. That power sometimes makes people think that they should be able to have everything that their heart desires, even if they cannot afford to pay for it. When you don't have enough money to pay for all of the things that you are buying, you have to make decisions as to what is most important to have. You have to divide things up according to wants and needs. Definitions are needed here. A "want" is something that you'd like to have, but that you can do without if you need to. A "need" is something that you cannot do without. Food is a need, but it is a need that can be filled by many kinds of food. Deciding to buy an expensive steak in order to fill your need for food would be a "want". Your need for food could easily be filled by many other foods that are less expensive. There is nothing wrong with having your need for food filled with your wants from time to time, especially if you can financially afford to do it. The trick is to be careful that you don't let your wants influence you into making decisions that are not in the best interest of your financial future.

Imagine that your family's household makes $5000 a month after taxes are paid. The list of wants and needs for the household might look something like this:

Needs	Wants
Mortgage/rent $1950	Video rentals
Electric/water/heat $360	Video game purchases
Car payments $500	Movies/bowling/entertainment
Clothing $200	Designer clothes
Food $500	Eating at restaurants
Retirement savings $500	
Telephones $250	
Gas/Insurance $350	

So far, on the needs side, the total is $4610. That leaves $390 to cover any emergencies that may come up like car repairs, school field trip expenses, work expenses, etc. If you ask your parents for money because you want to buy the newest video game or another pair of designer jeans, you may feel that it should not be a problem for you to get it. You may think that since there is $390 leftover to spend (and that you just want a small piece of it), you should be able to get what it is that you want. It would probably be a surprise for you if the answer from your parents is "No". Why in the world would they say "No" when they have an extra $390 that is available to be spent? The answer is that just because they have the money and CAN spend it, does not mean that they SHOULD spend it, especially when it comes to the wants. You always, ALWAYS pay the needs before you pay for the wants. One day, you may find that the extra money comes in handy to help pay for the increases that always seem to happen on the "needs" side of the list.

It doesn't have to cost more to be worth more.

Just imagine that you are shopping for a new television because your old one stopped working. You walk into an electronics store in order to see what you have to choose from. As you walk into the television area, you notice a 32-inch flat panel TV that has the clearest picture that you've ever seen in your life. Just then, a salesperson from the store comes up behind you and says the words that are music to your ears: "Beauty isn't it? Can I help you take this one home with you today?" You say, "That would be great!" He then says, "It's our most popular TV, and we only have two of them left, so you should get it today if you really want it." You can't stand the thought of losing out on the most popular TV, so you spend all of the money that you have saved in order to buy it. You give little thought to how much you paid for the TV as you read the directions for how to mount it onto your bedroom wall. There is no question that you will enjoy the TV, but was it worth it to spend all of your money in savings in order to buy it? Was there a way that you could have gotten a TV and still had money left over? Yes, there was.

Sometimes it pays, and pays big, to shop around before buying. Back at the store, you probably didn't notice that there were other 32-inch TVs for sale. It might have surprised you to learn that one TV could cost $900, and another one of the same size costs only $700. It might further surprise you to learn that sometimes, the only difference in what 2 products have to offer is the name on the tag (and the price). Sometimes, you can find the exact, identical product in one store, but see it priced $150 less at

another store down the street (or on the internet). Is one worth more because it costs more? No. If a TV goes on sale at the time of some holiday sale, and is priced lower by the store in order to sell it, is it worth less? No. Sometimes, stores put coupons into the newspaper or magazines in order to get people to come into their stores to spend money. A 10% off coupon means that you would save $90 on a TV that usually costs $900. Can you think of things that you could do with an extra $90? You can spend it on something else that you need or save it for something else that you might have to buy another day.

Before you think that this only applies to expensive things, let me show you how it works with small things at the grocery store:

Wonder® whole grain bread $2.69	Store brand bread $1.99
Minute Maid® OJ $3.49	Store brand OJ $2.99
Smucker's® jelly $2.19	Store brand jelly $1.69
Bob Evans® sausage $3.49	Jimmy Dean® sausage on sale $2.49
Ball Park® beef hot dogs $4.39	Gwaltney® beef hot dogs $3.99
Pillsbury® sugar cookies $3.49	Store brand sugar cookies $2.50
Morton's® salt $.89	Store brand salt $.69
Crisco® vegetable oil $4.59	Store brand vegetable oil on sale $2.39
TOTAL: $25.22	**TOTAL: $18.73**

This is a small shopping list but the savings is already $6.49. You have to eat every day and every week. What could your parents do with that extra money every week?

Just because you choose to look the other way, doesn't mean that they will.

There are many people who wish that it didn't cost money for material things. Until that day comes (if it ever does), the reality is that the majority of things DO cost money. That includes having a cellular phone, going to the doctor, living in a house or apartment, food, and having electricity in your house or apartment. All of those things cost money. A lot of companies allow you the use of their service first, and bill you for it later. That means that the doctor sees you first to tell you how to get better, and then they expect you to pay for their help before you leave their office (or make a promise to pay for it soon). You may figure to yourself that the doctor saw 10 patients in the hour that you were there, meaning that they saw about 80 patients that day (8 hours X 10 patients). You may figure that the doctor will be okay with not getting your money since he will get the money from 79 other people. Same with your cell phone company who has millions of other customers. What's the harm in one person not paying their bill? No big deal, right? They won't miss the money, right?

Whether they will miss the money or not is not important. What is important is that you gave your word that you would give them money in exchange for them giving you cell service, medical advice, a roof over your head, or electricity in your home. How would you feel if you gave them money, and they decided to take it and not give you what you asked for? It's a safe bet that you wouldn't like it. It's no different than you using their stuff and not paying them for it. Let me tell you what can happen when people do that.

Let's say that you promise to pay for your cell phone service, and don't. The company asks you for the money nicely, and then not-so-nicely when they see you are ignoring them. You figure that they will get tired of asking you, and you might be right. You might be more determined NOT to pay them than they are to get you to pay. Just because they stop calling or writing you doesn't mean they've forgotten you (or what you did). I'll tell you something else too. They like to warn their friends and help them out so that they will be spared the headache of possibly having the same problem from you. A credit bureau is a place where the cell phone company, the doctor's office, the electric company, the book club company, the car company, the rental office, and many other companies can exchange information about how you pay your bills. The cell phone company says to the credit bureau, "Hey guys guess what? Alex didn't pay me for her last month of service. She still owes me $50. Write that down." You may decide to get another cell phone months later. You are smart enough to know that your old company hasn't forgotten what you did, so you call another one. The new company will take your social security number and ask their pals at the credit bureau for the report on how well you have kept your promises to pay other companies. In all fairness, they don't keep just bad information... good information will be there too, if you kept your promises to pay. Want to know how long? The good information could stay on your report forever according to Experian.com (one of the credit bureaus). Most of the bad stuff stays on your report for at least 7 years, but can be as much as 15 years depending on the type of bill you had. By the way, there are THREE credit bureaus in the United States, each of them reporting all of the financial information that they can find out about you. If your report is mostly bad, companies probably won't give you credit, because your "promise to pay" won't mean much to them. Your past decisions and actions will mean more than your words if you didn't pay when you promised you would. When your words match your intentions, you have what is called "integrity", which according to my dictionary means "strict personal honesty" (from the same The American Heritage Dictionary). Once your creditors see

that you have integrity, they will be more eager to extend (give) more credit to you. More on that in the next section.

Note: It is important to regularly check to make sure that the information on all three of your credit reports is correct. You should check them at least once per year to be safe. The only way to have information removed from your credit file is if it is found to be incorrect. Information is power: Be informed about what's on your credit file. Give your parents the contact information for the credit bureaus that is contained in the back of this book. Help them to be informed too.

Be true to your word (trust = credit).

So, we already discussed how your decision not to pay a bill one day can follow you for many years later on your credit report. Besides avoiding a bad credit report, there are many reasons why it can benefit you to be true to your promises to pay. When you make a promise to pay for things, it is important to pay when it is due and in the amount that you said you would pay. Almost every bill has a due date, which is the date they would like to be paid. There is no harm in paying before the due date, or even on the due date. But if you pay after the due date (even one day late), you can get charged a late fee. Sometimes, it is a percentage of the bill amount, and sometimes it is a set amount like $25 or $50 dollars. That late fee is a penalty for not paying on time, and that late payment can get reported to… yes, you guessed it… the credit bureaus. If your bill is for $50 and they are expecting that amount, and you only send in $25, technically your bill was not paid on time, and you will likely be charged a late fee. You do not get to decide how much you feel like paying on your bill, although you are able to ask the company if they will make some other arrangements with you. They may say yes, or they may say no. For the most part, your decision to pay $25 to the cell phone company and spend the other $25 on a video game will likely result in a late fee getting charged and a bad mark on your credit report. Will that video game give you as many years of excitement as the number of years that the late payment will be on your credit report?

Also, there are things that you may want to buy later in life that you will have to get a loan in order to buy. A car, motorcycle, a student loan or a house are some examples. People who have records of sometimes paying on time (or at all) and sometimes not, will have a harder time getting approved for credit. Credit is something that is earned, and it doesn't come automatically. Say you want a fancy car that costs $20,000. You saved up $5000, and want to get credit to pay the other $15,000 to the car dealer. You apply for the credit, but because you have a habit of sometimes not paying your bills (or paying late) and only sometimes paying them on-time, you are told one of the following:

1) You are only approved for a loan for $5000 instead of the $15,000 you asked for. They think you might pay it back, but they aren't sure because you don't always pay on time (or at all), so they decide to minimize their risk (minimize means to reduce). This means that you have to get a different car that costs less.

2) You are approved for the full $15,000, but they still think you are risky, so they charge you 19% interest for the loan. Your parents got a car last year and got a loan with a 3.9% interest rate. Most car loans are for 5 years (they can be for less time), so the difference in interest is:

$15,000 @ 19% for 5 years= $389.11 monthly X 60 months = $23,346.60

$15,000 @ 3.9% for 5 years= $275.57 monthly X 60 months = $16,534.20

The riskier loan will cost $6812.40 more money! All because of decisions that you made years ago…

3) The car salesman walks you over to the used car lot and shows you cars that are $4500. He tells you that you aren't approved for credit, and can only buy something if you pay for it all using cash.

Do you now see the benefits and power that comes with being true to your word and paying back what you owe? People are more likely to help you to get what you want when you show them that you say what you mean, and mean what you say. That includes your friends that you may need help from one day. Think they'll lend you a dollar for a soda when you still owe them money from the last 5 times that you borrowed and didn't repay?

Choices you make today will likely affect your tomorrows.

I hear a few of you saying that you just won't get any credit. You won't get any credit cards, you'll buy a used car with cash, and you'll pay for everything with cash. That'll put an end to all of that credit nonsense, right? Wrong. Car dealers and loan officers aren't the only ones who check your credit report. Here are a few others:

1. Rental offices and landlords. You don't have to be thinking of buying something in order to have your credit report checked. Lots of landlords (people who own houses and apartments that are available for you to rent in exchange for money) and rental offices pull your credit report before deciding to rent to you. Doesn't matter whether you are trying to <u>buy</u> something or borrow it (rent). Just like you decided not to pay your cell phone bill… you could easily decide to stop paying your rent. A landlord could decide not to rent to you, or ask you to pay for two month's (or more) rent before you move in (because they think you are risky).

2. Car insurance, home or renter's insurance. Credit risk means that you sometimes may participate in risky activities. Risk means possible loss. Insurance companies don't want you to lose anything, because that means that they will have to pay for it (reason you have insurance is to repair or replace the item you insure if something happens to it). Car insurance:

pays to have your car fixed if it gets damaged in an accident. Insurance companies figure that if you don't care whether or not you pay your bills, you may not care if you park your car in a safe place, or you may not care if you drive 90 miles per hour (greater chance of an accident, which means they're more likely to have to pay to repair/replace).

3. Companies/employers. When it comes time to get a job, they may pull your credit report because it gives them a good idea of what kind of worker you may be for them. If you don't care about paying your bills on time, are you going to care about coming to work on time or completing projects when they are due? Or worse, if you owe a lot of money to companies and don't have enough to stop them from going after you to collect it, will you be tempted to try to steal money from the company in order to stop the bill collectors? Again, not my rules...

Not having any credit on your report, while not terrible, is not so great either. Companies and potential creditors (those who could possibly give you credit) need to see that you can handle credit RESPONSIBLY. So, not having any credit (good or bad) doesn't show that you know how to promise to pay, and then pay back in-full and on-time. The key is to mean what you say (keep your word) and to be responsible. You never know who will be interested tomorrow in what you are doing today.

Cash is the king (but credit is queen).

Many people have been taught to only buy what they can pay, for using their cash. Having the cash to buy something is great, because once you buy it, it is yours and you won't owe any more money to anyone for it. Although credit can be a wonderful tool to help you achieve your goals in life, it also has the power to seriously damage your life and relationships when it is not used with care and responsibly. As a result, people are often advised not to spend more than they make. In some circumstances however, using only cash will not be possible, and using credit will make perfect sense.

A mortgage company ("t" is silent) grants people a loan when they want to buy a house. A house will be one of the largest purchases that you will ever make. Whether it's a condo, townhouse or a house, the cost for it can range anywhere from $60,000 to $600,000 (or more). Not many people will have that kind of money sitting around available to plunk down for a place to live. Even if they did, they wouldn't want to spend all the money that they have all at once (need to save some for emergencies, repairs, etc). They will need to get a mortgage loan. Loan companies decide how much to lend to you based on your credit and your ability to pay (<u>income:</u> money you earn from jobs, work and investments). The more money that you have that you can put down towards the purchase of the house (money that the mortgage company won't have to pay), the lower the interest rate that you will be charged for the loan (because you are taking some of the risk away by putting up your own money), and the more likely it is that you will be approved for the loan (if you have decent credit already). Same with a car loan, by the way. Think of the loan

company as a friend who is lending you the money to buy what you want because they see that you are serious about getting it (you saved for the down payment= your contribution), your credit report says that you pay back what you owe, and you make enough income to afford the monthly payment.

The loan company is not going to approve you to buy a house that costs $3000 a month if you only make $5000 total per month. You wouldn't want them to either. Houses go up in value (how much they are worth) as time goes by. You don't want to go into a buying situation knowing ahead of time that you cannot afford it (and may therefore lose it). Mortgage companies will take back the house (and car companies will take back the car) if you stop paying for it. You will lose your house/car, and most (if not all) of the money that you used to put down the initial down payment on it. Foreclosure (loss of a house as I described) is a horrible thing to have happen. So is the repossession (taking back) of a car, bankruptcy (when your bills overpower your income and you can't pay them anymore), and financial ruin from not "living within your means" (spending more than you make).

Strike up a good balance between the two: Credit, used in moderation (not extreme) and responsibly, can be a wonderful companion to the cash that you have available to use. Together, the king (cash) and queen (credit) can help you achieve your financial dreams.

**A note about credit reports: It is important to know that when a company is deciding whether or not to extend credit to you (and how much if they do), they take a look at your complete package. Though a company may request a copy of your credit report to help them make the decision, their decision is not always based SOLELY on what's on your report. So, the credit bureau does not decide whether or not to approve your loan or credit application. The bureau just lays out the facts about your accounts (as your previous creditors have reported them) and how you have paid on them.

Pay less now, or pay more later.

Having a credit card in your wallet gives you choices. One of the biggest choices that you have is whether or not to buy something that you may not have the cash to buy at this time. You may go to a website on the internet and see something that you would love to buy. You look at your bank balance (record of how much money you have in the bank) and see that you only have $100 available. You know that you have another paycheck coming, so more money will be available to you as soon as you get paid again. Is it a good idea to go ahead and buy it using your credit card? Let's explore it.

Two people can go to the same store and buy the same jacket. If one person pays for it using cash or a debit card, and the other uses their credit card, they may not be paying the same price for the jacket. Here's why:

Cash Purchase   Credit Purchase

$175 $175 on credit card = $175 or more

When the credit card bill comes in the mail, you have a certain amount of time to pay off the balance before you get charged an interest charge. If you don't pay the full balance, your interest rate will determine how much interest gets charged to your account. If you used your credit card to pay for the purchase price of the jacket ($175) your total balance would be $175. Your bill will give you that balance, and give you the option of making a minimum payment of perhaps $10 by the due date.

If you pay that $10, your payment won't be late (if you pay on-time), but you will get charged interest for not paying the full balance. You get a new statement every 25 days or so. When the next statement comes out, it will show your $10 payment, but it will also show another addition to your balance: interest. That is the money that you pay the credit card company for carrying your balance until you decide to pay it all off. If you go to www.consumercredit.com, you will find a credit card interest calculator that can show you how long it will take for you to pay off that $175 jacket charge by just paying that minimum payment of $10. It will take 20 payments, they will charge you about $24 in total interest, and it will take you 1.66 years to pay it off

A credit card with a 15% interest rate means that you could end up paying a total of $199 for that $175 jacket (and taking up to a year and a half to do it). You'll pay more in interest if you decide to use your credit card to pay for anything else during those 1.66 years. Have a credit card balance of $500 and the interest jumps up to $289, the number of payments becomes 79 and it will take you 6.58 years to pay it off (if just paying the minimum payment). Do you really want to pay for a jacket, jeans, sweater, boots and a watch for the next 6.58 years? Will you even be wearing that jacket 6.58 years from now?

Don't just pay the "minimum payment", or you'll be paying a lot more for the items that you purchased with your credit card.

15.

Credit is not your money.

One of the most difficult things for teens (and some adults) to understand is the whole concept of that rectangular piece of plastic called a credit card. It is so simple to pull out a credit card when it's time to pay for something. The person at the store gives you the total amount for what you want to buy, you pull out the credit card and hand it to them, and then they swipe the card across a magnetic reader. It usually only takes about 15 seconds or less for the cashier to hand you a pen and ask you to simply sign your name. Seconds later, you are on your way out of the store, carrying bags containing what you just bought. People sometimes pay for things with their credit card without giving any thought to whether or not they can really afford those things.

Credit can be your best friend, or your worst nightmare. The wonderful thing is that you have total control over which it will be for you. Credit doesn't just do things on its' own without your consent. You make the decision whether to buy something now, or wait until later. You decide whether to pay for something today using a credit card, or wait until you've saved the money in your bank account to buy it using cash. Credit is not free or additional money. Please read that again. If a credit card company decides to make $5000 available to you for you to make purchases, that does not mean that you have now earned $5000 to do with as you please. It means that you have $5000 available for you to use, *at a cost*. We talked in the last section about credit interest charges, which are extra charges over and above the purchase price of the item you buy using a credit card. Buying on credit is like taking out a loan. Since it is such, you should think about whether or not you would take out a loan in order to buy "X". If you have the money, or expect to have the money soon, in order to pay for what you charge on your credit card, then no problem. Credit would just be a convenient way for you to spend what you already have (or are soon going to have). But if you're charging $2000 worth of things each month but are only making a total of $1000 each month, you may soon find yourself in financial trouble or shocked to find that it will take years to pay off your rising debt.

What is "your money" is the money that is connected to a debit card. Debit cards allow you to make purchases up to the dollar amount that is available in your bank account. If you have $500 in your checking account and deposit (add) your $400 paycheck, your available bank account balance will be $900, and your debit card will allow you to make purchases that total up to $900. Your purchase limit is the available amount in your account. They are very different from credit cards. You can't buy more than you have money to pay for, which makes debit cards a lot safer to use for some people.

One other thing to mention: it is okay to borrow money today to buy things that will be worth more tomorrow or that you absolutely need today. It is okay to borrow money to buy a house (house should be priced reasonably). It is okay to borrow money for student loans for your education (is an investment in your future so that you can learn more to earn more). It is even okay to borrow money in order to buy a car that you need in order to get to work or handle your responsibilities (again, a reasonably priced car). It's not advisable to borrow money in order to buy things that you <u>think</u> will be worth more, later. Borrowing money in order to purchase the first release of a video game system is not advisable. Be reasonably sure that it will be more valuable later before taking out a loan (credit) to buy it now.

Will I still love it tomorrow?

With all of this talk about the value of items, the cost of credit, and the importance of saving, there is something that stands out as being important to think about when considering a purchase. Whatever it is that you are thinking about buying (clothes, toys, TVs, video games, etc) should go through two tests. We already covered the first test: The needs vs. the wants test. The second test is simply to give some thought to whether you will have the same feeling about the item tomorrow as you are having about it today. In other words, have you thought it through to make sure that you're going to be thrilled about having it next week or even tomorrow?

Impulse buying is what happens when a person buys something that they didn't plan on buying. Going into a store to buy a frozen pizza for dinner but coming out with the pizza AND ice cream that was advertised for sale, freshly-made donuts and two candy bars displayed at the checkout line is impulse buying. Going to look at a used car that you can afford and coming home with the flashiest, fanciest new car on the sales lot…. is impulse buying. After the thrill and excitement of buying that item has left you, will you still be glad that you spent the money that you did in order to buy it? Will you still think it was a good idea to buy "X"?

Stores and advertisers (companies who spend money to deliver a message to you on the TV, radio, billboard, newspaper or magazine about an item or service that they'd like you to try and buy) want you to spend your hard-earned money on what they have to sell. The more

that you buy, the more money they make. Their goal is to try to get you to spend as much of your money as they can. They don't care whether you can afford it, whether or not you need it, or whether you have another one similar to it at home already. The messages that they try to deliver to you will show the item looking as big, beautiful, shiny, useful, and cool as possible in the hopes that you will run out to the store and buy one or more of them.

It's almost like a tug-of-war with your money. They are on one side trying to get your money, and you are on the other side, hopefully trying to be careful with your spending so that you have money to take care of your needs, future emergencies, and things that you know that you really want to buy. In the end, what you spend your money on will be YOUR choice. Some things that you buy will cost you money to return if you later decide to take it back, and some things will not be returnable once you open them. So, you should choose carefully.

Make sure that when you are choosing to buy something, it is something that you need or something that you REALLY want.

You have to crawl before you walk.

One final note about credit before moving onto other topics. It's worth mentioning here that building credit is a lot like learning how to walk. Children are not born knowing how to walk. They actually aren't born knowing how to crawl either. They just kind of lay around not knowing how to do much of anything except lay there, virtually helpless. Several months after birth, something happens to most babies. After they've learned to roll over, they soon master the fine art of crawling around. They soon learn to sit up on their own without any help, and it's not long before they learn to pull themselves up in order to get a better view of the world. Many a parent has been both excited yet terrified as they've watched their child take their first steps while trying to balance themselves without falling down. Watch out when that child learns that they've got the tools (their legs) to take themselves wherever they want to go. Once they've figured that out, they are literally off and running as fast as their legs can take them. It's not much different from credit, or a lot of other things in life, really.

Credit does not just happen overnight, nor are you born with the ability to charge things using credit. You also don't start off knowing how to build or use credit. Credit is a privilege that is granted to you over time as you demonstrate that you have the self-control to use it wisely and carefully. Everyone starts out with nothing connected to their credit but their name, address and social security number. What happens from that point going forward will be up to you. Wish all that you want, but you won't start out being able to buy a new car or a house when you are a teenager. You will start off small by getting credit from a cell phone company or

even a dentist's office who decides to let you make your payment later. Pay them on-time, and you can perhaps move up to getting a secured credit card with a small credit line. A secured credit card is one that uses your money that is held in a savings account as collateral (backup) in case you decide not to pay your bill. Your credit limit will in most cases be the amount in the savings account. $500 balance in savings, $500 credit limit. Secured credit cards are wonderful tools for helping to build your credit because they give you a chance to prove that you understand the whole concept of paying what you owe ON-TIME (responsible credit use). The more time that goes by with you using credit responsibly, the more credit that will be granted to you. The beautiful thing about being responsible with your credit use is that others will want to give you credit, and those who are already giving you credit will give you more of it. Many secured credit card companies will raise your credit limit once you demonstrate that you are responsible. Though you still only have the $500 in savings, they can raise your limit to $750, $1000 or more. A day will come when they decide to give you back your savings balance (with interest), and tell you that they trust that you'll do the right thing with your account.

The point is, that there is not really a shortcut to building good credit, just like there wasn't one when you learned how to walk. Take your time and exercise your muscles to make them stronger so that they'll be secure and powerful when it's your turn to run out into the financial world on your own.

If you fail to plan, then you are planning to fail.

When you think about it, whatever it is that you seek to accomplish with your life will have a starting point and an ending point. The start happens when you decide to do or get something and then you move towards achieving what you want. Seems pretty simple. Sometimes the end point will be exactly where you thought that it would be, and other times, it will be at a different place altogether. Let's say for example that you wanted to get from point A to point Z. You would most likely think of point A as the start, and point Z as the finish (or end). Thinking of it though, there are many letters in between A and Z. And there are many ways that you could get from A to Z. The easiest way would seem to be to go straight through, but you could go fast, slow, or fast and then slow. There will usually be more than one way to get to where you are trying to go. Making the decision to go after what it is that you want in the world is a large part of the work. Actually taking steps to move towards what you want is even bigger. And while it is important to just "do it", it is equally important to have a plan for how you will do it.

When talking about finances and saving, it is a good idea to devote time to creating a budget. A budget is really a plan that helps to guide you in the direction that you want to go in terms of wealth. A budget can help you to see what you have coming in (income) and what you have going out (expenses). A budget is very helpful in showing you how well your income is covering your expenses. It also shows you how you are spending your money every month. When you look at the things that you are spending your money on, you will learn which things are important to you (you will see where you spend the most money). Budgeting can help you to get control of your expenses. You may decide to cut your expenses in an area (like entertainment, eating out at restaurants, or buying coffee three times a day) to help you save money once you see what you are spending on things. It can basically help you to set and then achieve your financial goals. Creating a budget can help you to find ways to save money for your wants, your rainy day fund, and your future. So how do you create a budget?

Create a chart with your income and expenses written on it. You will want to keep track of your income and expenses for at least two weeks or more so that you can really see how and where you are spending. Make sure that you keep all of your receipts so that you can record the money that you are spending. That will include money spent on gas, a place to live, food, entertainment, coffee, bus or train money, telephone charges, clothes, jewelry, computer disks, school supplies, money spent at the bowling alley, and money spent downloading songs from the internet. If you spend 50 cents on something from a gumball machine every Monday and Friday, record it in your budget book. Your book or journal doesn't have to be fancy, it just needs to be readable to you, and have enough space to be able to write down all of the amounts of money that you earn and spend.

When you are finished tracking your spending habits, you will have a very clear picture of why you are in the financial situation that you are in (good or not-so-good). The great part about budgeting is that it can help you to turn things around, even if things are not-so-good. You will hear it mentioned several times in this book: Information is Power! Once you get it, use it.

It could happen to you.

In your lifetime, you will be a witness to many accidents. Though you may not see how they happened, you will see the results of and effects from them. You may ride by a house or apartment that has black burn marks outside the openings where the windows were before they got blown out by a fire. You may see a story in the newspaper about a hurricane, earthquake, tsunami, tornado, or even a torrential downpour of rain that does significant damage to a small (or not so small) city. You will likely see people hurt and cars demolished as a result of a car accident. Things happen- sometimes when you least expect them.

It's not that you should expect for any of these unfortunate events to happen to you. Hopefully, none of them will. Most people who have been involved in an accident didn't see it coming. So while there is little that you can <u>do</u> to prepare for an accident, there is something that you can <u>have</u> to be ready for one if it does happen: Insurance.

There are many types of insurance. Auto, boat and motorcycle insurances protect those vehicles. If you have proper insurance coverage, you will be protected if someone else damages, steals or destroys your car, boat or cycle. It also protects you if you caused an accident. The right insurance policy can cover your item, the other person's item and medical care for both people if they get hurt. Medical insurance protects your body in case it gets sick or damaged. Dental (teeth) and vision (eyes) coverage protects those specific parts of the body. Life insurance provides money to your family after you die. Home insurance protects your house and what's in it. Renter's insurance protects your belongings in your apartment. There are many other different types of insurance.

They all work basically the same way.

You must pay money (premium) in order to keep the policy in effect. If you suffer a loss, you tell the insurance company about it and they investigate how and why the loss happened. The details of what your policy covers will determine who the insurance company pays, if they pay, and how much they'll pay. In the case of medical, dental and vision coverage, your doctor will be the one giving the insurance company most of the information. If you don't pay the premium, you lose the insurance coverage.

Yes, insurance is an extra bill and expense. No, insurance is not required for everything. Sometimes, it will be your choice whether or not to have some types of insurance. The importance of insurance is quite simple: Not having it can devastate and wipe you out financially, eliminating your financial wealth. A person who has a car accident and does not have any insurance may have to use their own money to repair the car or buy a new one; use money to repair or buy a new one for the other person in the accident; use money to pay for medical bills of one or both people; and possibly use money to repair or replace personal belongings that may have gotten damaged in the accident.

Which would you rather do? Pay some money on an insurance policy, or spend your life savings trying to repair the damage caused as a result of the unexpected? You may not need ALL types of insurance, but it's smart to have SOME.

Love what you do...the money will follow.

An interesting thing happens when you ask teenagers today "What do you think your life will look like when you grow up?" You may or may not have given any thought to that question yet, but if you have, you may have answered like a lot of people:

- ❖ "I'm going to be rich, have a wife and two kids, and be happy."
- ❖ "I'm going to be like Bill Gates and make millions of dollars."
- ❖ "I'm going to be a pro baseball star so I can make lots of money."

More and more, it seems like the focus for people is all about money, and how much of it they can get so that they can buy whatever their heart desires. Ask your parent if they ever heard the saying "Money makes the world go round", and I'm sure that the answer will be "Yes". It's not necessarily true though. Believing that money will make everything better or make your life more fulfilling is what drives people on a mission of accumulating (collecting) as much money as possible, regardless of what they have to do to get it. This includes choosing a job or career simply because of how much money one can earn in that field.

As of the writing of this book, Microsoft Corporation's Bill Gates is supposedly worth billions of dollars. Pro baseball players are making anywhere between hundreds of thousands to millions of dollars per

year, depending on the team and how good the team owners think they are. I have no doubt that Bill Gates is doing exactly what he loves and what he wants to do. He thought of the idea of creating a company that does what Microsoft does, and he decided to do it because it's what he loved. I'm sure that there are plenty of baseball and basketball players that absolutely love the game that they play. Many of them are probably amazed at the money that they are making for doing what they love to do. For them, it may not feel like a job. They would do it even if they didn't get paid all of that money, because they are not doing it for the money. Then there are people whose only reason for pursuing something is the money that they think it will bring to them. It seems like things are getting a little mixed up. Part of the problem is that as kids, you're told that the things that you love to do is called "Playing", while the things that you are made to do by your parents is called "Work". Most adults go to "Work" in order to make money to pay the bills for food, clothing, shelter and other wants and needs. That is the message that my son sometimes gets as he hears me tell of having to work for a client in Baltimore. What I hope that he sees however is his mother doing what she loves to do, and getting paid money to do it.

Loving what you do is powerful because when you do, you get energized and excited to do the work. Your energy and enthusiasm will help you to give your best efforts, and it has a way of rubbing off onto other people (customers, coworkers and bosses). Customers will be more willing to buy from you, coworkers will be more willing to help you get your work done, and bosses will be more willing to pay you top dollar to keep your enthusiasm around to help motivate others and keep the customers buying. Work can take up so much of your day, so it would be unfortunate to spend all of that time doing something you don't love. Even if you're not doing what you love, can you find a way to love (or even like) some part of what you have to do for your job? Ask your parents what they would like to do, even if they weren't going to get paid to do it? That will give some direction and guidance for learning how to get in touch with what you love to do.

Money isn't everything.

While we've talked about earning money, saving money, budgeting, investing money and protecting your money and possessions, it important to mention that money isn't everything. Yes, money can be a tool that can help you to reach and achieve your hopes, dreams and goals. While money doesn't necessarily make the world go round, unfortunately in these days and times, the lack of money can sometimes make your world dark (if you have none to pay for electricity for lights) and extremely challenging (if you have none to pay for food so that you can eat healthy). Still, despite all of the things that money CAN do, there are things that it can't do.

Money really provides a way for one person to exchange it for something else that they need (or want). Money doesn't have to be in the form of coins and paper money. In some other cultures, it is measured by beads, rocks or even stones. I won't pretend to guess where money was created and used for the first time. I'll let you look that up if you really want to find out. Here are some of the things that money can't do:

❖ Can't buy you health (can just help you manage it)

❖ Can't buy respect for yourself

❖ Can't buy true friendships (those don't cost money)

❖ Can't buy you character (character is one of the things that makes you unique)

❖ Can't buy you happiness (though you can buy things to make you think you are happy for some time period)

❖ Can't buy you joy

❖ Can't buy you love

❖ Can't buy you true peace of mind

Most people, if they found out that they were going to die soon, would not think to themselves "Oh, I wish that I had more time in order to make more money." They would more than likely think of doing all of the things that they hadn't made time to do (or hadn't gotten around to doing). This would include things like spending time with family and friends, smiling, laughing, loving and experiencing all that life has to offer.

The life that lies ahead of you will truly be a journey filled with greatness and discoveries that you can only imagine. Along the way, take time to remember what is truly important that you have access to right now. Try not to get so caught up in making money that you forget the things and people around you that don't cost a dime! You can enjoy those things NOW.

You can't take it with you.

We live in a time where there are a record number of successful people living in the world among us. Despite the number of people who have managed to create prosperity and wealth in their lives, there are also large numbers of people who just simply don't have the same story to tell. There are people who don't have money for food, clothing or shelter, and some who don't have insurance to fix the things that are causing them pain in their bodies. It is truly sad to see a person sleeping out on a park bench with all of their belongings piled into a metal shopping cart beside them. It is also sad to see a family doing the best that it can for its' members, but still not being able to feed everyone more than one meal a day. There are people who use their kitchen ovens in order to try to heat their house because they don't make enough money to get the furnace (heater) working. There are others who are losing the teeth in their mouth because they cannot afford the luxury (treat) of going to a dentist in order to save them from decay. What does any of this have to do with you, you ask? You may think that the answer is "Nothing", but I'm hoping that I can change your answer to "Something".

Despite the fact that many people who are experiencing hard times are people that you may never see or meet, it doesn't mean that you should turn your back and simply say, "It's not my problem". If it were you or your family that was going through some of those hard times, would you want people to say "It's not my problem" and turn their backs on you in your time of need? Having compassion for others, understanding their situation, and doing what is in your power to help, are all things that

make us human. I'm not going to get into whether or not animals and insects have feelings and compassion for other animals and insects. I'm going to stick to the fact that humans do have the ability.

Philanthropy, according to my trusty dictionary, is "The effort to increase the well-being of mankind, as by charitable donations" (p.514). Sharing your money or time, or donating food and clothes in order to help other humans is a considerate and kind thing to do. As the saying goes, "Do unto others as you would have them do unto you". When you are fortunate enough to be able to not only have your basic needs and necessities in life met but also some of your wants, why not reach out and share some of your good fortune with someone who has not had such good fortunes in life? We all have the ability to be a philanthropist. That word isn't just reserved for the millionaires in the world who are in positions to give a bit more freely (and more) of their money and time than perhaps the average person can. That word can be proudly worn on the sleeve of the person who participates in canned food drives, who donates money to a charity of their choice, who donates clothes to a homeless shelter, or who donates their time to help children who don't know how to read, learn to read.

If everyone would reach out to help, no one would be without. No need to be afraid of giving some of what you have away, because there is enough for everyone.

Treat others as you would like to be treated.

Most people have heard this saying before, so it's probably not new to you. You are however probably wondering why it's in a book that deals with financial things. There's a very good reason why it is here.

Every day at electronics stores across the county, people are buying everything from TVs and computers to MP3 players and music CDs. People are paying for those items with cash, checks, debit cards and credit cards. There is nothing remarkable about the cash and debit card transactions because the money will either leave your wallet or your account at the time of the purchase. But the check and credit card transactions are different.

A person with a checking account has the ability to walk into that store and buy a TV by writing a check for it. The store will have no way of knowing whether the check that was written for $800 is able to be turned into cash by their bank (the money is in the bank to cover the check). Let's say that the person who wrote the check doesn't have the money in the bank to cover the amount of the check. The store would then be in a situation where they no longer have the product (TV) and they don't have the money for the product either. In this case, the person literally got something (TV) for nothing but the cost of the gas to get it home from the store. I just want to ask you: If you or your parents owned an electronics store, would you want people to be able to get something for nothing from your store? The same thing for the person who pays using a credit card. The credit card company sends the money for the TV to the store on your behalf (you signed telling them it was okay to do it). You will then owe the credit card company the money for the TV. If you decide to stop paying your credit card company, then it is they who will suffer the losses while you got something for nothing. My next question to you is: How would you feel if you lent money to someone and they never paid you back?

Think about that when you go through life and you have financial transactions with other people and companies. By the way, it also applies to the places where you live. Treat other people's property with the same care that you'd want them to give to yours. If you are renting the place where you are living then the landlord or company that owns the place had to spend their money to buy the place, and spends money for taxes, insurance and repairs for the place. If you were your landlord, how would you want the house or apartment to be treated? Wouldn't you want the person who lives in your building to treat it with care?

Another way of putting this is: Do unto others as you would like them to do unto you.

True friends want what is best for you (not just for themselves).

Everyone likes to have a good time. You go out with your friends to the movies, to the mall, to restaurants, on road trips, and on vacations (like spring break). Most of those activities require some amount of money that has to be spent by someone. When you're out with a group of people, there's certainly nothing wrong with one person deciding to pay everyone else's way as a treat or nice gesture. What a treat it is to have your dinner, movie tickets or gasoline for your car paid for by someone else.

It's not such a treat though when one person is the one who is usually doing the treating. So I can hear some of you saying that you don't see anything wrong with having someone else usually being the one to pay your way. Think about this for a minute: are you friends with that person because they have a great friendship to offer you, or are you friends with them because you don't have to reach into your own wallet when you are around them?

Rather than go into a discussion of what makes a person a true friend, I'll simply ask you to think for yourself about how you would feel if you had friends around you who never reached into their wallets to pay for anything because they usually waited for you to pay? Even if you have the financial ability to always pay the way for your friends, would you want to have that be the foundation of your friendships? Wouldn't you want to know that your friends ARE your friends because of a mutual respect and genuine "like" for one another?

One last thing to mention about friends and money: You may think that one of the nicest things that you can do for a friend is to either loan them money or co-sign for a loan for them. Co-signing is what you do when one person's credit is not satisfactory for them to get a loan or an extension of credit on their own. When you co-sign for someone else, you become financially responsible for that loan and the repayment of the loan or credit account. That means that if your friend or relative decides to stop making payments (or does any of the things that caused them to have unsatisfactory credit), you will be responsible for paying their bill (even if YOU don't have the car, motorcycle or TV that THEY bought using the credit). When you co-sign for someone else, your credit file becomes connected with theirs. When the late or missed payments from that account gets reported to the credit bureaus, it will get reported on your credit file as well as that of the person who you co-signed for. Is your desire to help your friend really worth the possible costs to you? There is a saying: You can't really help someone else who doesn't want to help themselves first.

Any friend who makes you co-signing for them or paying their way for them a condition of your friendship is not really your friend. Your true friends would not make what you do (or don't do) for them a condition of the friendship. They want what is best for you, not just what is best for themselves.

Things aren't always the way that they look.

One only needs to look at a television or a magazine to see that the general public seems to be fixated with having all of the things that they see other people with. If you stand in line at the grocery store, you'll see magazines that show movie stars and celebrities with expensive clothes, fancy cars and spectacular homes. It's hard not to find yourself sometimes saying "I wish I could have what they have". It doesn't just happen when you see movie stars and celebrities though. There will be people who live near you, go to school with you, or work with you who have things that you don't have. It could be a nice car, an expensive pair of shoes, or a costly game system.

There are people who choose to spend more money on electronics than they spend on clothes. Some spend more on their car than their home. Some spend more on clothes than on anything else. If you look at something that someone has and think that the person must have a lot of money to be able to afford it, you would be making an assumption. The definition of an assumption is "a statement accepted as true without proof" (The American Heritage Dictionary, 1983, p.42). It is always interesting to see someone driving a car that costs $60,000 pull up in front of their apartment that is located in a part of town where the rent is only $400 per month. It is of course their choice if they want to spend all of that money on an expensive and fancy car, and spend as little as possible on the place that they live.

Just because someone is carrying a purse that costs $300 doesn't mean that they are rich. Just because someone lives in a huge house

that looks like a mansion, does not mean that they are a millionaire. Just because someone is driving a fancy sports car, it does not mean that they have the money to afford it. Just because a person owns something, it doesn't mean that they can actually afford to keep it. There are a lot of people who live what is called "paycheck to paycheck". That means that they spend all of their money from one paycheck, and can't pay for anything else until they get their next paycheck. Sometimes they spend their paycheck in their minds before they even get it into their bank account or hands. It would probably surprise you to hear that a number of people who actually are millionaires don't live their lives that way.

People think that all millionaires buy expensive clothes, watches, the latest greatest cars and the biggest houses. People assume that if a person is worth a million dollars, then he or she probably spends money on whatever they want to buy. While some millionaires do spend their money on those things, many don't. There are many millionaires who dress in "regular clothes", drive cars that are many years old, wear a $50 watch on their arm, and live in "regular sized houses". If you saw them walking on the street, you would never guess that they are millionaires.

There was a story about a woman who worked every day of her life cleaning the clothes and houses of other people. When she died, a college was very surprised to hear from her lawyer that she had left money in her will to the college in order to provide students with a scholarship to attend that college. Many people thought that the amount of money would be hundreds or possibly thousands of dollars. Imagine everyone's surprise when they learned that the actual amount was over a million dollars!

Things are not always the way that they look.

Help! Somebody stole my identity!

Unfortunately in the world today, there are people who will not have your best interest in mind…only their own. There are some people that don't want to work for what they need and want in life. They'd rather get things quickly and easily by stealing them from others. They may try to steal from you one day. It's another one of those things that you most likely won't see coming. Someone may try to steal your money, or someone may try to steal your identity.

You may wonder how someone can steal your money if it's sitting in a bank or credit union account. You would probably be able to guess quickly that if you have a debit card that is linked to your bank account, then all a thief needs would be the actual card to be able to buy things using the money from <u>your</u> account. Remember, use the debit card and the funds get immediately reserved and are no longer available to you? Then there is the ATM card that you can use to withdraw money from a machine. In order to take money out of the machines, you need to use your personal identification number (PIN). Though you may have trouble remembering the PIN, it is absolutely critical that you NOT keep your PIN anywhere near or on your ATM or debit card. You must keep the two separate so that it will be difficult for a thief to access the money in your account. There is additional information that you need to keep safe.

Your social security number is that unique number that belongs to ONLY YOU. There won't be anyone else that has the same number as you. You must guard your number with your life and keep it safe. You should not carry it with you in your wallet. You should not throw away any piece of paper that has your number on it (you need to shred it so that a thief can't piece it together), and you shouldn't leave any papers out that have your number on it. Why is it so important to guard that nine digit number? A thief can use your personal information (name, address, date of birth, and social security number) to open up accounts in your name. They can open up a new credit card or a bank account, get a new cell phone plan, get a mortgage, buy a car, rent an apartment or even get a job using your personal information. Why would that be a problem for you? Just imagine that someone gets a credit card using your information and then buys everything in town using the card, never paying one cent on the bill. Who will they come after and whose credit file at the bureaus will be damaged? YOURS! The worst part about it is that you probably won't know that it has happened to you until you get a call from a bill collector about it, or you try to open an account yourself and are told that you have problem credit (that you didn't know anything about).

So what can you do to protect yourself from identity theft? First, be very careful who you give your personal information to. Next, guard your personal information carefully, and keep it just about under lock and key (preferably in your head or at home). Your social security number is one of THE most important numbers in your life, and it should be memorized and stored in your mind instead of being with you on a piece of paper. Trying to recover from the damage of identity theft is not impossible, but it can sometimes take a lot of time and work on your part. The best way to handle it is to do what you can to prevent it. This lesson is extremely important. So important that you should do what you can to help to educate your friends and family on some of the things that they can do to protect themselves from identity theft. They will thank you for this:

❖ Anyone who gives you credit or a bank account should have your correct name, address and phone number (so you can keep track of your accounts)

❖ Don't lend your credit or debit cards out to anyone

❖ Report lost or stolen cards as soon as possible (helps to limit the damage that the thief can do, which limits your potential loss and time spent trying to correct the thief's damage)

❖ File a police report if you are a victim of identity theft

❖ Check your bank and credit accounts for charges you didn't make. Also, check your credit report (all 3 credit bureaus) at least once a year to make sure there aren't any errors or accounts that YOU didn't open on it.

❖ Don't give your personal information out to someone you don't know (especially on the internet or in an email). People send out random emails pretending to be your bank or credit company (saying they have a problem with your account) or lying to you by saying that they need your information to be able to give you a prize.

❖ Don't throw away or recycle papers that have your personal information still on them (that are readable). People will do what is called "dumpster diving" to get your information (look through the trash for information).

❖ Only deal with companies that are trustworthy (especially when shopping on the internet). Also, some credit card companies can offer you a disposable credit card number that is good for one transaction only (so that your actual credit card number doesn't get transmitted over the internet or to a site or person that means you harm).

❖ Don't pick your phone number, house address, date of birth or social security number as your PIN.

Information is power, and it will be your best defense against identity theft.

Books I Recommend:

For Teens/Tweens:

The Kid's Guide to Money Cents. By Keltie Thomas. Kids Can Press, Tonawanda, NY. 2004

Financial Literacy for Teens. By Chad Foster and Misty Elliott. Rising Books, Conyers, GA. 2005

It's Not What You've Got! By Dr. Wayne Dyer and Kristina Tracy. Hay House, Carlsbad, CA. 2007

ForAdults:

Don't Spend Your Raise: and 59 Other Money Rules You Can't Afford to Break. By Dara Duguay. Contemporary Books; Chicago. 2003

Spend Well, Live Rich: How to Get What You Want With the Money You Have. By Michelle Singletary. Ballantine Books; New York. 2004

Rich Dad, Poor Dad: What the Rich Teach Their Kids About Money. By Robert Kiyosaki and Sharon Lechter. TechPress; Arizona. 1998

The Millionaire Next Door: the Surprising Secrets of America's Wealthy. By Thomas Stanley and William Danko. Longstreet Press; Georgia. 1996

Other books by Marlena Jareaux

26 Things to Teach Your Parents
(Available on amazon.com, 26thingstoteach.com and through Baker and Taylor.)

Coming soon:

26 Environmental Things to Teach Your Parents

Additional Resources

Credit bureau contact information:

The Big Three in the USA:

www.TransUnion.com or 1-877-322-8228

www.Experian.com or 1-888-397-3742

www.Equifax.com or 1-800-685-1111

You can order a free copy of your credit report by going to www.annualcreditreport.com

Many other countries have either a Public Credit Registry or a Private Credit Registry. Some don't have either. The "Big Three" listed above also provide services for other countries in the world, including Canada.

Websites with additional information:

www.mymoney.gov

www.jumpstart.org

www.jumpstart.org/madmoney (reality check to see how much "life" will cost you)

http://hsfpp.nefe.org/students/index2.cfm?deptid=15

www.360financialliteracy.org

THE END.

ORDER FORM

Fax or send your order to:

Inspired by the Beach Publishing
P.O. Box 174
Simpsonville, MD 21150-0174
Fax: 240-782-4222 • Phone: 877-411-TIME

SHIP TO:

_____   _____
Name   Company

_____
Street Address

_____
City   State   Zip

_____   _____
Telephone   email

BILL TO (If different from SHIP TO):

_____ Attn: _____
Company/School

_____
Street Address

_____
City   State   Zip

_____
Telephone

PAYMENT OPTIONS:

❐ Purchase order Attached: #_____
❐ Check enclosed **(make payable to _Inspired by the Beach Publishing_)**
❐ Paypal payment **(send payment to _info@corridorconcierge.com_)**

Quantity	Unit price	Total
	10.95	
Shipping	Add 10% Minimum $4.00	
	TOTAL